CCSS **Genre** Exposito

M000288979

Essential Question
How does weather affect us?

Weather All Around

by Deborah November

1 What's the Weather?

Have you ever noticed that people love to talk about the weather? Sometimes it is hot. Sometimes it is cold. Sometimes it is nice outside, and sometimes it is not! Some weather is harsh. Different parts of the United States have different weather.

In some places, it is hot most of the time.

Many places in the United States have four seasons.

Seasons

Some places have four **seasons**. The weather changes with the season. Winter is cold. It may snow. It is **breezy** and rainy in the spring. Buds appear on the trees and flowers start to bloom. Summer is usually hot and sunny. The fall is crisp and clear. The colorful leaves fall off the trees.

Hurricanes in the East

The Northeast has four seasons, and so does much of the Southeast. Hurricanes can happen in these areas. These dangerous storms bring heavy rain and strong winds. Hurricanes happen more often at certain times of year.

Hurricanes and Seasons

Hurricanes form over the Atlantic Ocean. They happen mostly in the summer and fall, when the ocean is warmest. As storms blow across this warm water, they become stronger. Some turn into hurricanes.

These scary storms even have names, such as Hurricane Ike or Hurricane Isabel! The first storms of the season get names that begin with the letter A. Later storms get names beginning with B, C, and so on.

The middle of the hurricane is called an eye.

One good thing about hurricanes is that we know ahead of time that they are coming. This warning gives people a long time to prepare. Sometimes powerful hurricanes can destroy homes. But with a warning, people can protect themselves. They can prevent damage to their homes. Some people cover their windows with wood so that the glass does not get broken.

What to Do in a Weather Emergency

1. Stay calm.
2. Seek shelter.
3. Wait for the alert that the storm is over before resuming normal activities.

People may board up their doors before a hurricane.

5

3 Great Plains Snow

The Great Plains, as you can probably guess from the name, is a very big place! It stretches all the way up the center of the United States and over parts of Canada. Most of the Great Plains is very flat and open. Areas that are flat can sometimes have a harsh weather event.

The Great Plains can be very windy.

Blizzards

Winter in the Great Plains brings snowstorms. A snowstorm happens when there is very cold air in the clouds. Clouds then collect cold water. There is also warmer air by the ground. When the warm air rises up into the clouds, it mixes with the cold water. Snow then falls out of the cold clouds. Big storms are called **blizzards**. The wind is strong and the temperature is very low during a blizzard.

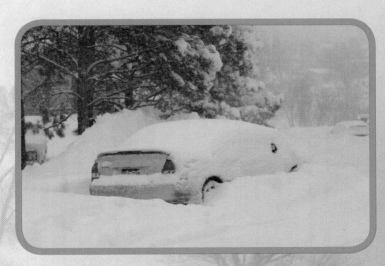

A blizzard is a fierce snowstorm that lasts for a long time.

As with hurricanes, we usually know that a snowstorm is coming. This gives people time to get ready. What should you do if a snowstorm is coming? You might have to stay home if there is a lot of snow. It is dangerous for cars or buses to travel on **slippery** roads. There might just be a snow day! On snow days, children stay home from school.

After the snow stops, you can use a ruler to see how much snow fell.

Emergency Planning

You should have an **emergency** kit ready in case of bad weather. Some of the things that should be in your kit are plenty of water and food that does not need to be cooked. A radio and batteries are also good things to have. An emergency kit will prevent the need to leave your home during the storm.

It is a good idea to have warm clothes and blankets in your emergency kit.

4 Midwest Tornado Watch

The Midwest has seasons like the Northeast. The weather is different during every season. It is often colder in the Midwest. It is also very windy, and tornadoes can happen there.

Tornadoes move very fast.

What Is a Tornado?

A tornado is a big, dangerous storm. It swirls around and turns in circles. Tornadoes, or twisters, happen most often in the spring.

Stay in a safe place until the weather radio tells you the tornado is gone.

It is a good idea to have a weather radio in your house. It can warn you that a tornado or other storm might be on the way. If a tornado is coming, your family should go into the basement. You can also go into a bathroom that has no windows. Staying away from windows and doors during a tornado is very important.

Weather Words

Do you know the difference between a *watch* and a *warning*? If there is a tornado *watch,* that means watch out. There might be a tornado. If there is a *warning,* a tornado is probably on the way.

5 Southwest Drought

The southwestern part of the United States is usually hot. Temperatures often climb above 100 degrees in summer. The weather here is also very dry. The seasons do not change much in the Southwest. A lot of the land here is desert. A desert is a very hot and dry place that does not receive much rainfall.

If there is not enough rain, plants can die.

Droughts

Sometimes in the Southwest there is a **drought**. That means that it does not rain for a long time. If there is no rain, people have to be careful not to use too much water. During a drought, the people who live in the Southwest hope that the rain will come soon.

Animals that live in the desert need very little water.

All kinds of weather can be beautiful. Every season has something special that you can enjoy. No matter where you live, or what season it is, enjoy the weather all around you!

The weather in Hawaii is sunny most of the time.

Summarize

Use important details to help you summarize *Weather All Around*.

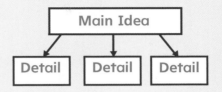

Text Evidence

1. How do you know *Weather All Around* is expository text? GENRE

2. What happens when there is a drought? Use details in the selection to support your answer. MAIN IDEA AND KEY DETAILS

3. Use what you know about antonyms to figure out the antonym of *nice* on page 2. ANTONYMS

4. Write about what items you would put in your weather emergency kit. Details from the selection may help. WRITE ABOUT READING

Compare Texts
Read about the colors in the sky during one day.

Colors in the Sky

Do you ever wake up very early? The sunrise is filled with beautiful colors. The sky sometimes looks orange through the clouds.

If it is not rainy, the sky turns bright blue after sunrise. On a rainy day, it looks gray.

Sometimes after it rains, you might see a rainbow. Can you name all of the colors of the rainbow?

Colors of the Rainbow

Some people remember the colors of the rainbow by remembering ROYGBIV. That stands for red, orange, yellow, green, blue, indigo, and violet!

After the sun goes down again, the sky is dark blue or black. Can you see any bright white stars in the sky?

Make Connections

How does the weather affect us every day?

ESSENTIAL QUESTION

How can the weather change the color of the sky?

TEXT TO TEXT

Glossary

blizzards *(BLIZ-urdz)* heavy, long snowstorms *(page 7)*

breezy *(BREE-zee)* windy in a nice way *(page 3)*

drought *(DROWT)* a period of very dry weather *(page 13)*

emergency *(ee-MUR-juhn-see)* something serious that happens all of a sudden *(page 9)*

seasons *(SEE-zuhnz)* four periods of the year that include winter, spring, summer, and fall *(page 3)*

slippery *(SLIP-uh-ree)* hard to stand on, often because it is wet or has ice on it *(page 8)*

Index

Focus on Science

Purpose To find out how weather affects us

What to Do

Step 1 With a partner, talk about the weather in different parts of the United States.

Step 2 Divide a piece of paper into four parts.

Step 3 In each part, draw a picture showing what the weather is like in a particular place. Label your picture with weather words.

Conclusion Talk about different types of weather with your partner. Discuss how they make you feel. Which type of weather is your favorite? Why?